MW01290558

Keep a Song in Your Heart

MUSICAL NOTES FOR DAILY DEVOTIONS

Jackie Freeman

WESTBOW
PRESS®
A DIVISION OF THOMAS NELSON
& ZONDERVAN

Copyright © 2021 Jackie Freeman.

All rights reserved. No part of this book may be used or reproduced by
any means, graphic, electronic, or mechanical, including photocopying,
recording, taping or by any information storage retrieval system
without the written permission of the author except in the case of
brief quotations embodied in critical articles and reviews.

This book is a work of non-fiction. Unless otherwise noted, the author
and the publisher make no explicit guarantees as to the accuracy of
the information contained in this book and in some cases, names
of people and places have been altered to protect their privacy.

WestBow Press books may be ordered through booksellers or by contacting:

WestBow Press
A Division of Thomas Nelson & Zondervan
1663 Liberty Drive
Bloomington, IN 47403
www.westbowpress.com
844-714-3454

Because of the dynamic nature of the Internet, any web addresses or
links contained in this book may have changed since publication and
may no longer be valid. The views expressed in this work are solely those
of the author and do not necessarily reflect the views of the publisher,
and the publisher hereby disclaims any responsibility for them.

Any people depicted in stock imagery provided by Getty Images are
models, and such images are being used for illustrative purposes only.
Certain stock imagery © Getty Images.

ISBN: 978-1-6642-4779-6 (sc)
ISBN: 978-1-6642-4780-2 (hc)
ISBN: 978-1-6642-4778-9 (e)

Library of Congress Control Number: 2021921402

Print information available on the last page.

WestBow Press rev. date: 10/23/2021

The Christian Standard Bible. Copyright © 2017 by Holman Bible Publishers. Used by permission. Christian Standard Bible®, and CSB® are federally registered trademarks of Holman Bible Publishers, all rights reserved.

Scripture quotations are from the ESV® Bible (The Holy Bible, English Standard Version®), copyright © 2001 by Crossway, a publishing ministry of Good News Publishers. Used by permission. All rights reserved.

Scripture taken from the New King James Version® Copyright © 1982 by Thomas Nelson. Used by permission. All rights reserved.

Scripture quotations taken from The Holy Bible, New International Version® NIV® Copyright © 1973 1978 1984 2011 by Biblica, Inc. TM. Used by permission. All rights reserved worldwide.

Scripture taken from The Message. Copyright © 1993, 1994, 1995, 1996, 2000, 2001, 2002. Used by permission of NavPress Publishing Group.

Scripture taken from the King James Version of the Bible.

Scripture quotations marked (NLT) are taken from the Holy Bible, New Living Translation, copyright ©1996, 2004, 2015 by Tyndale House Foundation. Used by permission of Tyndale House Publishers, a Division of Tyndale House Ministries, Carol Stream, Illinois 60188. All rights reserved.

TO
Joy Thomas Price
(1933-2018)

*"There are many virtuous and capable women in the world,
but you surpass them all!"*
Proverbs 31:29, NLT

Momma,
You have blessed many people, but no
one more than me, your daughter.

Keep a Song in Your Heart shares the wisdom
and witness of the generations of my family
who blessed me. Besides Momma,

Perry Price (1928-2008)
Isabella Davis Price (1888-1953)
Dolph Daniel Price (1879-1956)
Nettie Wild Thomas (1903-1991)
Herman Thomas (1900-1990)

On a hot summer day, a cluster of women gathered at the Onsted Senior Center to hear *Cynthia Furlong Reynolds* talk about writing. I was among them. A friendship and my new career blossomed from that day onwards. She has been a mentor, writing coach, editor, and collaborator on this and other projects. Many thanks to her.

Prologue

Sing a Joyful Song!

Music wove and flowed and coursed through my life even before I was born, thanks to the incredible musician I called Momma. Joy Thomas Price was well named. Joy filled her life—and mine—with joyful praise and worship songs. My earliest memories center on Momma sitting at her upright piano as she played selections from the old Free Will Baptist Hymn Book and the stacks of sheet music piled nearby. Momma and her gospel songs taught me Scripture, God's deep and abiding love for us all, and a reverence for the awe-inspiring power and beauty of Christian music. That piano bench never could contain all Momma's music. Nor can it possibly contain all the memories I cherish of my mother and her love for music and the Lord.

America's gospel music tradition emerged in the 1920s, the decade before Momma was born. It blends sacred hymns with spirituals, jubilee quartet songs, and African-American devotional music, spiced by rhythmic jazz, blues, and harmonics. For a century, gospel music has soothed sorrows, proclaimed joys, preserved stories, and inspired new paths, always reminding listeners that God is the source of our lives and salvation.

Keep a Song in Your Heart is a legacy project inviting you to join with the generations of my family as we explore the wisdom those Southern gospel masterpieces impart. As Momma played and I sat beside her and sang, I was mesmerized by the magic I was witnessing. Gospel music makes memorizing Scripture easy, and gospel music clarifies and highlights Scripture's wisdom in new and exciting ways. In these devotionals, I share how the greatest gospel works inspired my family—and I hope it does the same for you. Thanks to modern technology, I can share the music itself with you via **Spotify**, a free computer/phone app.

Momma's old upright piano sets the stage for us. I hope you find Joy and joy in your personal journey, as I have.

Hugs,
Jackie

Playlist

Keep a Song in Your Heart
And I'll keep you in tune!

Day 1: "I Know Who Holds Tomorrow" by Alison Krauss, The Cox Family—I Know Who Holds Tomorrow

Day 2: "Born to Serve the Lord" by Greater Vision—Not Alone

Day 3: "Had It Not Been" by The Gospel Heirs—Had It Not Been

Day 4: "Because He Lives" by Carrie Underwood—My Savior

Day 5: "Just A Closer Walk With Thee" by Patsy Cline—Here's Patsy Cline

Day 6: "Then I Met The Master" by the Booth Brothers—The Best of The Booth Brothers (LIVE)

Day 7: "It Is No Secret" by Bobbie Mason, Jake Hess—Gaither Album, It Is No Secret

Day 8: "Teach Me Lord To Wait" by Gold City - Revival

Day 9: "Sheltered In The Arms Of God" by The Rambos—Rambos Collection

This is how to use this Devotional as we spend time together:

My journey began with the **Music**, which triggered the **Memory,** which inspired each devotion's **Message,** and my **Movements,** or actions. Your journey might begin with my **Message**, which triggers one of your **Memories,** inspired and augmented by the **Music**. My prayer is that these **Messages** result in **Movement**—actions—on our part. You might consider four simple questions at the end of each devotion.

1. How does the **Message** speak to you?
2. What **Memory** of yours does it trigger?
3. What phrase from the **Music** resounds most powerfully in your ears?
4. *What **Movement** or actions can you take based on the Message?*

Message....

Memory...

Music....

Movement...

Day to Day

Day 1

I Know Who Holds Tomorrow

Words and Music by Ira Stanphill

Five years ago, I never would have imagined I would be a widow, an orphan, and an empty nester. A lot has happened to me during these years. What about you? Are you where you thought you'd be? Or do you sometimes think you are living someone else's life—certainly not the one you planned for yourself?

No matter how close I felt to Jesus, I have wept the cries of King David: "How long?" "Why?" "Where are You, God?" "Why didn't my life turn out as I hoped and expected?" "Why did my husband and parents have to die and leave me here, alone?"

I now understand the working power of crying out to God, especially when I don't understand my circumstances. When I want to run away from God, I cry out to Him instead. Why? Because He hears and He cares so deeply "Give all your worries and cares to God, for He cares about you" (I Peter 5:7, NLT).

I gradually realized that my God shares my pain, my lonely nights, and my fears. He hears my prayers, and He cares—deeply.

Amid my losses and pain, God has opened new doors for me: a writing career I never expected, more time to spend with my grandchildren, new friendships, travels around the world. I'm claiming the verse from James 1:17 (NIV): "Every good and perfect gift is from above, coming down from the Father."

Do you wonder how you got to this moment and time?

Are you worried about tomorrow? Let me tell you, **I Know Who Holds Tomorrow,** and I know who holds my hand. I'm learning to breathe again. No longer do I feel suffocated by my anxieties and worries. My identity does not rely on who is in my life, but on whom I live for: Jesus. My confidence is in the Lord. Jesus is the one who stands by me, holding my hand these days. He understands and wants to hold your hand, too.

> Heavenly Father, so much of life puzzles us. We know You care for us, and that reassurance should be enough. Please give us the calm and peace that can only come from Your touch. Thank You, Lord. Amen.

Message..._____

_____

_____

_____

Memory..._____

_____

_____

_____

Music..._____

_____

_____

_____

Movement_____

_____

_____

_____

Day 2

Born To Serve The Lord

Words and Music by Bud Chambers

Isn't it exhausting to be the center of your own universe, always performing, always listening for the applause? You feel like you have an armful of plates spinning in the air, realizing they will all come crashing down at some point. At times, I have been so full of myself that I left little room for God.

As my parents' only child, I was the apple of their eyes, their little princess who could do no wrong. But that was not exactly the reality, as my cousins could tell you. This "kissing cousin" was a *biter*. Yes, yours truly resorted to biting kids to get them to do what I wanted them to do. I shudder at the memory.

Believing I was so perfect, I just knew God needed me to control my little corner of the world for Him. Even after I came to know Christ as my Savior, I wanted to orchestrate everything and everyone. My control factor was out of control.

So, you can imagine my surprise when I learned in Ephesians 2:10 (NLT): "For we are God's masterpiece. He has created us anew in Christ Jesus, so we can do the good things he planned for us long ago." We were **Born to Serve the Lord**. He has plans for us.

We all have a decision to make. Do we follow God, or do we struggle with Him for control? I soon recognized I needed to get out of His way, get into His Word, and get in step with

His will for my life. God helped me bite my tongue more and listen without having an agenda.

Are you fighting the Holy Spirit for control in your life? Do you think you've got a better idea? Many people in the Bible who knew God's plan for their lives turned their backs and walked away from Him. We also read accounts of individuals who stopped, listened, and heeded the words of Jesus. Mark 8:34 (NLT) tells us, "Calling the crowd to join his disciples, he said, 'If any of you wants to be my follower, you must turn from your selfish ways, take up your cross, and follow me.'"

What will you choose: your selfish way or God's way? God is at work. He has a plan for you and me. Your musical score is written. Do you choose to walk in harmony or discord?

> Heavenly Father, make us instruments of Your melodious composition. Help us grow more like You with each passing day. Amen.

Message..._____

_____

_____

Memory..._____

_____

_____

Music..._____

_____

_____

*Movement*_____

_____

_____

Day 3

Had It Not Been

Words and Music by Rusty Goodman

I am a book lover. Books live on my shelves for many years, eager for me to revisit them. I especially love historical fiction, because novels transport me to different places and times and introduce me to heroes and heroines with grit, determination, and exciting destinies.

But one book, in many translations, surpasses all others in my collection: the Bible. From early childhood onward, I memorized passages that have inspired me, sustained me, empowered me, and comforted me.

However, God's Word didn't come alive for me until I made a pilgrimage to the Holy Land.

Until then, Bible stories were just epic stories starring Omar Sharif as Lawrence of Arabia or Charlton Heston as Moses. The Ottoman Empire and Fertile Crescent were topics I memorized to pass a test in school. So, I expected my trip would explore the ancient sites I had read about. I didn't expect my trip would thrust me *into* the story.

Now, I believed and taught that Jesus was the Son of God. But I never *lived* the Bible until I gave the Holy Spirit control of my life. That happened as I looked over Calvary, where the real living, breathing Son of God died for me. There, at last, I realized He was real, not a character in a novel. Were my early years wasted? No. God planted the seed for me to grow, but it wasn't until I grew in His Word that I discovered the power of

His plans for me. "Man does not live on bread alone, but on every word that comes from the mouth of the Lord" (Deut. 8:3; Matt. 4:4, NIV). "The word of God is alive and active" (Heb. 4:12, NIV).

Had It Not Been for God's love for you and me, **Had It Not Been** for a place called Calvary, **Had It Not Been** for a man called Jesus, what would we be? _Lost_. But "God so loved the world that He gave His only begotten Son, that whosoever believeth in Him shall not perish but have everlasting life" (John 3:16, KJV). That is not just a story. It is the Gospel. It is the Truth. And our lives should be an open book attesting to this Truth.

> Heavenly Father, thank You for giving us Your Word, "explaining spiritual realities with Spirit-taught words" (I Cor. 2:13, NIV). May we "shine… like stars in the sky as [we] hold firmly to the word of life" (Phil. 2:15-16, NIV). Help us grow spiritually, like the mighty cedars of Lebanon, when we allow Your Word to transform our lives. Amen.

Message... _____

_____

_____

Memory... _____

_____

_____

Music... _____

_____

_____

Movement _____

_____

_____

Day 4

Because He Lives

*Music by William J. Gaither. Words
by William J. and Gloria Gaither.*

Never underestimate the power of a praying grandmother. As a little girl, I witnessed Grandma Thomas's example of Christian living. I watched her read her Bible, take part in Bible studies, and lead the women's Prayer Band at church. Prayer was on her lips; God's Word filled her heart.

Recently, I discovered letters Grandma Price wrote before and after my birth. Like all great correspondence, these letters offer insights into the woman who knew me, loved me, but never met me. Isabella Price died in North Carolina the winter following my birth.

Grandma Price wrote in pencil on small tablet paper now yellowed with age. Her words encompassed events of the day, the health of family and the farm, the weather, and, of course, updates on her children, who had scattered around the globe. She always requested prayer and thanked God in her salutations for all His blessings.

The month before I was born, she instructed my parents, "Always keep hold of the Lord's hand. I pray that God will be with Joy in carrying and delivering that little darling that you are expecting." Just before her death, she wrote about me: "I have her picture on the dresser, and I'm praying for God to take care of that little baby, can't wait to squeeze her. Take good care of my baby darling."

The Apostle Paul also wrote priceless letters full of guidance and love for people he would never meet. II Cor. 1:5 (NIV) says, "For just as we share abundantly in the sufferings of Christ, so also our comfort abounds through Christ." In other words, **Because He Lives**, we all can face our tomorrows courageously, for "life is worth the living just because He lives." My grandmothers had the calm assurance that their grandchild would overcome any adversity by turning to Christ. How did they know? The same way the Apostle Paul knew: because of the manger, the cross, the empty tomb, and their personal relationship with our living Savior. In Matthew 28:20 (NLT), Jesus promises, "Be sure of this: I am with you always, even to the end of the age."

What about you? Have you been blessed with a role model who pointed you to Jesus at an early age? Or have you been a pioneer, finding your way to Christ through His Word and His followers? Either way, know that Christ cherishes you, guides you, comforts you, and strengthens you.

> Heavenly Father, we thank You for Christ and the role models He placed in our lives. We thank You for the realization that **Because He Lives**, we can face uncertain days fearlessly. Make us aware of opportunities to demonstrate Your love and presence to others. Amen.

*Message...*_____

_____

*Memory...*_____

_____

*Music...*_____

_____

*Movement*_____

_____

Day 5

Just A Closer Walk With Thee

Origin Unknown

Have you found yourself out of breath as you race to catch up, trying your best not to be left behind?

I have. As a child, I tried to go as fast as I could, but I could not equal the stride of my Grandpa's long legs on our daily jaunts in the neighborhood. Herman Thomas stood over six feet tall, and to me, his first grandchild, he appeared to be a gentle giant. He was a quiet man who loved his family, his God, his country, and his Detroit Tigers. He was also a generous man who always looked for ways to help others. As we walked "uptown" to the Kresge store or Cunningham Drug Store, this little girl tried desperately hard to keep up with him.

Grandpa walked everywhere. Even though he worked for Ford Motor Company for more than thirty years, he never drove a car. His grandkids could all tell you stories of walking with Grandpa and how each of us, as little squirts, ran to catch up. The neighbors said they could set the time on their watches when Brother Thomas passed their houses. He enjoyed walking and greeting his neighbors, seeing what they were up to, and asking if they needed his help. That's the man Grandpa Thomas was.

Grandpa came to know Christ as Savior when my mother was a little girl, and from that moment, he instilled in his family the importance of following God's commandments. As he walked, I wonder if Grandpa thought about II John 1:6 (ESV): "This is love, that we walk according to His commandments."

Following in Grandpa's footsteps, I've learned over the years what the Lord requires of us: "O People. The Lord has told you what is good, and this is what he requires of you: to do what is right, to love mercy, and to walk humbly with your God" (Mic. 6:8, NLT).

God has given us the Holy Spirit to guide us in **Just a Closer Walk with Thee**.

> Heavenly Father, day by day guide us as we try to walk just a little closer to You. We know Your promises are true, and we want to fulfill the purpose You have for our lives. Amen.

Message..._____

_____

_____

_____

Memory..._____

_____

_____

Music..._____

_____

_____

*Movement*_____

_____

_____

Day 6

It Is No Secret What God Can Do

Words and Music by Stuart Hamblen

Grandparents can be the sugar and spice and everything nice in a child's life. Mine certainly were. A grandparent's presence—or absence—is crucial to future generations, especially these days, when we see more and more grandparents raising grandchildren. How would you describe your relationship with your grandparents?

One of my earliest recollections is sitting with my grandmother on her front porch swing in the days before we had screens to swipe or video games to entertain us. Grandma would say, "Climb on up here. Let's sit awhile." We waved at neighbors or watched the kids play across the street. And we invented games.

Playing "I spy with my little eyes," rhyming games, and perhaps a little "storytelling make-believe" filled lazy afternoons. On that swing, I learned my left hand from my right hand. I learned that pumping my legs would make the swing go higher. And I learned to count, thanks to the links on the chain holding that swing in the air. Grandma made learning a pleasure. Always.

And we always sang. I stood by her side and belted out the chorus of whatever song we chose. In those moments, life was a stage, and I was the star of the show. The next-door neighbor, Mrs. Dean, would always get a chuckle out of my crescendo. No one slept while I sang.

Stuart Hamblen wrote **It Is No Secret What God Can Do**, the first song I remember hearing Grandma sing. Her head tilted upward, as if she were singing to the angels, and her soft-spoken voice invited me to linger on each word and note. Then the chorus rang out her message:

It is no secret what God can do. What He's done for others He'll do for you. With arms wide open, He'll pardon you. It is no secret what God can do.

Grandma wanted me—and you—to know her Jesus and His promises. She held Proverbs 22:6 (MSG), to be true, "Point your kids [grandkids] in the right direction – when they're old they won't be lost." Do you have role models in your life like my Grandma, who joyfully showed a love for Jesus and passed that legacy down to you? Do you see yourself as a role model to others who need to know what God has done for you?

> Heavenly Father, help us be an encouragement to someone today. Show us ways that we can sing out the Good News of Your love. Amen.

Message..._____

_____

_____

Memory..._____

_____

_____

Music..._____

_____

_____

*Movement*_____

_____

_____

Day 7

Then I Met The Master

Words and Music by Mosie Lister

*In the beginning was the Word, and the Word was
with God, and the Word was God."
John 1:1 (KJV)*

Bibles can reveal our deepest concerns, greatest joys, perplexing questions, and *Aha!* moments on their worn and well-thumbed pages, if we let them.

The first Bible I received had a black faux-leather cover with my name engraved in golden letters. I was thrilled when I carefully turned the brand-new tissue-thin pages that smelled like wisdom. I carried that Bible to church, memorized Scriptures, and relied on it for Bible drills. But the pages remained pristine.

During adolescence, my Thompson Chain-Reference Bible offered a broader perspective for understanding God's Word; unfortunately, my walk with the Lord broadened only a little. As a bride, I carried a small white Bible down the church aisle, but afterward, my designated pathway took many detours and dead ends. But **Then I Meet the Master** and longed to know him better. I read more and wrote notes in the margins, recording important dates, questions, and cross-references.

Today we can read Bibles on tablets, smartphones, and laptops. We can listen to audio apps as we bicycle, wash kitchen floors, or climb mountains. A variety of good translations—such as KJV, ESV, CSB, NIV, NLT, NKJV, and *The Message*—all proclaim Jesus Christ as our Lord and Savior. Only through Him will we find salvation by grace through faith. "For the word of God is alive and active" (Heb. 4:12, NIV). Remember, "All Scripture is God-breathed and is useful for teaching, rebuking, correcting and training in righteousness" (II Tim. 3:16, NIV).

Bibles provide instructions on meeting our Maker: "You shall love the Lord your God with all your heart and with all your soul and with all your might...And these words... shall be on your heart. You shall teach them diligently to your children and shall talk of them" (Deut. 6:5 -7, ESV). People everywhere are desperate to meet our Master and understand His Word.

Occasionally, ministers preparing funeral eulogies ask to see the loved one's Bible for insight into their lives. No one could doubt that my friend Maggie used her Bible well; it held dates of her readings, sermon notes, a prayer list, a tattered photo of her late husband, a lace-edged hankie, and encouraging messages. Her Bible never gathered dust on a shelf. What about yours?

> Heavenly Father, we are forever grateful for Your Word, which paves the path straight to You. May we never allow it to gather dust. You knew us long before we were born; we want to know You just as intimately. We are thankful to be called a child of the Master's. Help us share Your Word with the world. Amen.

Message..._____
_____

Memory..._____
_____

Music..._____
_____

Movement_____
_____

Day 8

Teach Me, Lord, To Wait

Words and Music by Stuart Hamblen

I've never been good at waiting. Are you? I am not one who takes a deep breath, relaxes, twiddles her thumbs, and waits for something to happen. No, I jump in and get to work. But sometimes when I go it alone, I really muddle things up. Can you relate?

As a young child, I'd pout, stomp my feet, or scream to get what I wanted. It often worked. Remember, I was that spoiled "only child" of two adoring parents. But sometimes, my impatience and tantrums did not work. "Time out," Momma announced, as she sent me to my room to think about what I had done. This was a precursor to a pattern I needed to learn—and apply—throughout my life.

The words found in today's gospel hymn, **Teach Me, Lord, To Wait**, appear in Isaiah 40:31 (KJV): "But they that wait upon the Lord shall renew their strength; they shall mount up with wings as eagles; they shall run and not be weary; and they shall walk and not faint."

As a child, I memorized this verse in the King James Version and honestly thought it was intended for someone else, someone who *liked* to wait around. They could renew their strength. I didn't need to; I was strong enough.

However, through deeper study, I find other Bible translations modify this word "wait" as it appears in Isaiah. Both the Christian Standard Bible and the New Living Translation replace "wait" with "trust." The New International Version uses the word "hope." Whatever the verb, this verse doesn't refer to sitting around or biding your time as you wait for God to act. No, we are to be *active*, not passive. We must WAIT and TRUST with anticipation, confident that God will respond at precisely the right moment—and in His perfect way. We must have confidence in God, and HOPE in anticipation of what He has planned—because one way or another, He intends us to work for His kingdom, not just passively wait for His kingdom to come.

Just like my childhood time-out, I need to WAIT, TRUST, and HOPE in the Lord as I renew my strength. This way, I can replace showing off with standing up for Him. I know I'll need that strength for the things He has planned for my life. You will, too!

I am growing up in the Lord!

> Heavenly Father, thank You for working in my life. I want to be strong in Your name, keeping my eyes on You. As the refrain records, "Let me be on this earth what You want me to be." Amen.

*Message...*_____

_____

_____

*Memory...*_____

_____

_____

*Music...*_____

_____

_____

*Movement*_____

_____

_____

Day 9

Sheltered In The Arms Of God

Words and Music by Dottie
Rambo and Jimmie Davis

Sheltered in The Arms of God might have been my mother's favorite hymn. She played it daily, and she often invited me to sit on the piano bench and sing. Occasionally she altered the timing, placing a hold on a particular note. This hymn often led us to discussions about the concerns on our hearts and minds. When storms were raging in my life, the line "I have no fear when Jesus walks beside me" opened the floodgates.

Music does that. It allows the heart and mind to become one. The coherence found in music, the harmony, demonstrates how to achieve balance in an unbalanced life. And when words fail, music comforts the soul.

The 23rd Psalm is a beautiful example of God's love for, and devotion to, His people. He assures us He will refresh our souls even when we walk through the darkest, deepest valleys. "Surely your goodness and love will follow me all the days of my life" (23:6, NIV). Psalm 91 is another source of comfort: "He will cover you with his feathers, and under his wings, you will find refuge" (91:4, NIV). God promises, "When they call on me, I will answer; I will be with them in trouble. I will rescue and honor them" (91:15, NLT).

Because He walks with those who call Him Lord, we can sing the chorus loudly and confidently: "So let the storms rage high, the dark clouds rise, they won't worry me." Learning to rely on God, not ourselves, is a day-by-day, moment-by-moment commitment. God doesn't just provide strength for tomorrow; He provides strength for *today*.

When our eyes, blinded by the views of this world, cannot see clearly the path set before us, remember: "Lord, you are my strength and my fortress" (Jer. 16:19, NLT). God protects us from the fray and "leads me [us] beside quiet waters" (Ps. 23:2, NIV). The next time you face storms and perils, shout the promise from Psalm 27:6 (MSG): "God holds me head and shoulders above all who try to pull me down. I'm headed for His place to offer anthems that will raise the roof! Already I'm singing God-songs: I'm making music to GOD!"

> Heavenly Father, thank You for offering us the shelter of Your arms, the protection of Your rod and staff, and the promise that we will dwell in Your house forever. May we, like the psalmists of long ago, raise our voices in Your praises every day. Thank You for the gift of music, so we may "make a joyful noise unto the Lord" in every season of our lives. Amen.

*Message...*_____

_____

_____

*Memory...*_____

_____

*Music...*_____

_____

*Movement*_____

_____

_____

Day 10

I Bowed On My Knees And Cried Holy

Written by Nettie Dudley Washington

Dreams are mysterious blends of imagination, worries, secret desires, and crazy scenarios. Has a dream ever seemed so real that when you awoke, you were stunned (and perhaps disappointed!) to realize you were dreaming?

I have a recurring dream that someone is calling my name, but when I turn, no one is there. I try desperately to identify the voice and the cadence of their speech. Nothing. Who is calling my name? Does someone need my help?

Dreams appear in many Bible stories. Joseph (Gen. 40) and Daniel (Dan. 1:17) received God-given foresight through dreams, and they changed the course of history. Conversely, some dreams warned of what could go wrong if someone abandons the way of God. Saul confessed to the prophet Samuel (I Sam. 28:15, NIV), "God has departed from me. He no longer answers me, either by prophets or by dreams."

I wonder if Nettie Dudley Washington dreamed about heaven before writing **I Bowed on My Knees and Cried Holy**? Perhaps the passage in Philippians 2: 10-11 (NIV), inspired the words in the chorus: "At the name of Jesus, every knee should bow, in heaven and on earth and under the earth, and every tongue acknowledge that Jesus Christ is Lord, to the glory of God the Father."

I'm sure you, like me, dream of meeting loved ones in heaven. When I sang the names Abraham, Isaac, Jacob, Mark, Luke, and

Timothy in the second verse of this song, Momma said she could imagine them welcoming us home. More and more of my loved ones, including my husband and parents, have passed from this life. I'm sure one day I will again hear Momma playing her piano. And I am equally sure that I will bow on my knees when I come face to face with Jesus, the One who died for us all.

Maybe author Nettie Dudley Washington felt disappointed after she woke from her dream about heaven. Thankfully, she put the words to music. Nothing can stop us from singing praises to God.

> Heavenly Father, today we bow before You and praise Your name. Thank You for words and music that remind us of the love and guidance You offer us every day. Teach us to listen closely and respond lovingly. In Jesus's Name, Amen.

Message..._____

_____

_____

_____

Memory..._____

_____

_____

Music..._____

_____

_____

Movement_____

_____

_____

_____

Day 11

Take My Hand, Precious Lord

Words and Music by Thomas A. Dorsey

Hearing familiar melodies and lyrics can transport me to other places, other times. Have you experienced the same phenomenon? The song **Take My Hand, Precious Lord** does that for me. I sing this song often at memorial services, knowing that the composer, Thomas A. Dorsey, wrote it in the depths of grief and loss, following the death of his wife, Nettie, and their newborn son.

I also sang this song for an audience of one, while sitting by the bedside of a sick neighbor. She was tired. She was weak. She was worn. But as I sang, she began to hum along, softly at first. And then we sang the chorus together. A smile appeared on her tired face, and tears rolled down her cheeks. We knew that her hope rested in Jesus. Jesus would be there to take her hand.

The words found in Psalm 23:4 (NIV) must have comforted Thomas Dorsey as they comforted me in sorrow-filled times. "Even though I walk through the darkest valley, I will fear no evil, for you are with me." Death is nothing to fear when you know Jesus.

My mother's sheet music for **Take My Hand, Precious Lord** records the key in which I sang and the dates of the memorials. Keenly aware of how emotional each funeral service was, Momma encouraged me to let God take the *words* of the song, not the way I sang them or the way she played them, to move people closer to Him. She was right, as usual. God certainly used the lyrics of **Take My Hand, Precious Lord** to draw me closer to Him, especially in times of grief.

Whose name do you cry out in your times of need? When he was ready to give up, Thomas A. Dorsey recalled something from his Sunday School days and sat down at a piano to produce this powerful hymn, his cry to his precious Lord. How inspiring to learn that a man torn by sorrow would allow the Holy Spirit to guide him in composing this masterpiece.

I'm grateful for the lives that have come in and gone out of my life. I'm thankful for melodies and lyrics written decades ago, that continue to draw us closer to God.

> Precious Lord, guide our feet and take our hands when You lead us home. And until then, remind us daily that because You are with us, we never need to fear any evil. Amen.

Message..._____

_____

_____

Memory..._____

_____

_____

Music..._____

_____

_____

*Movement*_____

_____

_____

Day 12

I Am Blessed

Words and Music by Jerry Goff

S poiled little girls want what they want when they want it. These same spoiled little girls grow up and expect the same thing—at least I did. I wanted to have it all—and have it all *now*!

I believed if I tried harder and worked longer, I could make all my dreams come true. WRONG.

Society's expectations of what we need and what is popular change all the time, and I soon learned I couldn't keep up with them. The saying "If you don't stand for something, you will fall for anything" describes many of us who try to accommodate this world.

I Am Blessed reminds us, "I have shoes, food, and shelter," so what more could I want? According to the world's standards, I am rich beyond measure. I have a loving family, a comfortable home, good health, and fantastic friends. I want for nothing. So, you can imagine how I felt when I read Psalm 119. At 176 verses, this psalm, the longest chapter in the Bible, used to intimidate me. But now as I read it, I realize God used the psalmist's words to remind me of what a blessed life looks like: "Turn my eyes away from worthless things; preserve my life according to your word" (Psalm 119:37, NIV).

Luke shows Jesus discussing the same issue with His listeners: "Are not five birds sold for two pennies? Yet not one of them is forgotten by God. Indeed, the very hairs of your head are all numbered. Don't be afraid: you are worth more than many sparrows" (Luke 12:6-7, NIV). Jesus continued, "I tell you, do not worry about your life, what you will eat; or about your body, what you will wear. Who of you by worrying can add a single hour to your life?" (Luke 12: 22, 25, NIV).

A blessed life results from knowing and obeying God's Word.

Psalm 119:5 (NLT) becomes my mantra: "Oh, that my actions would consistently reflect your decrees!" The author reminds us that joyful, satisfied people search with all their hearts to discover His will in their lives. They walk in the path set by God—not fashion designers or advertisers—and they are eternally grateful for what God has done.

> Heavenly Father, help us live a life according to Your Word, not our world. You give us all we need, and so much more! We want to live a life of gratitude for what You have done for us. Daily remind me how **I Am Blessed** because of Jesus. Amen.

Message..._____

_____

_____

Memory..._____

_____

_____

Music..._____

_____

_____

Movement_____

_____

_____

Day 13

Restore My Soul

Words and Music by Mosie Lister

In the first *Rocky* movie, the camera zooms in on Rocky Balboa as the boxer races up the seventy-two stone steps of the Philadelphia Museum of Art. When he reaches the top and turns to face the city he loves, he raises his arms in a joyous salute. With grit and persistence, despite overwhelming odds, the underdog beats the champion.

We all like to root for the underdog, especially when his or her struggles mirror our own. I've felt like Rocky on more than one occasion. Just when I thought I'd "made it," life took me on a detour. When the difficulties of life caused me to spiral out of control, I felt helpless.

I cringe at the times God opened a door for me, but I followed my ego and pride instead of my God. Too often I listened to the prodding and praises of others and found my validation there, foolishly "walking in my own wisdom."

Instead of relying on my strength, I need to reach out to the nail-scarred hands of Jesus to **Restore My Soul**. Perhaps you do, too. Lamentations 5:21 (NLT) states our overwhelming need: "Restore us, O Lord, and bring us back to You again. Give us back the joys we once had."

How do we begin the process? By relying on God, not our own wisdom. Habakkuk reminds us in verse 3:19 (CSB), "The Lord my Lord is my strength; he makes my feet like those of a deer and enables me to walk on mountain heights." The book of Psalms is full of similar reminders: "The Lord is my strength and my shield" (28:7, NIV); "The Lord gives strength to his people" (29:11, NIV); and "God is our refuge and strength" (46:1, NIV). Perhaps the most powerful promise of all comes from Proverbs 3:5-6 (NIV): "Trust in the Lord with all your heart and lean not on your own understanding; in all your ways submit to him, and he will make your paths straight."

We can trust that God will give us victory in our battles. With His strength, we can run like Rocky Balboa: sure-footed, dancing for joy as we reach new heights. We know who stands in our corner of the ring—our God!

> Heavenly Father, renew in us a sense of Your strength. When our struggles seem overwhelming and victory seems improbable, may we trust in You, not our own understanding, knowing that You alone can restore our souls and make our paths straight. Amen.

Message..._____

_____

_____

Memory..._____

_____

_____

Music..._____

_____

_____

*Movement*_____

_____

_____

Day 14

I'm Feeling Fine

Words and Music by Mosie Lister

Do you jump out of bed in the morning, eager to start your day? Or are you grumpy before (or even after) your morning coffee?

I'm a morning person. I guess it's my temperament. So, no wonder I struggled with a husband who only grunted in the morning, followed by a quick kiss on my cheek as he headed off to work. I had to learn that all the fretting in the world will fix nothing. When I can wake up after a sound sleep, with birds chirping outside my window, I feel a fresh sense of joy about each new day.

Scripture tells us that joy is a state of being, while happiness comes and goes because it's based on our circumstances. According to Nivine Richie in UnlockingtheBible.org, "joy," "rejoice," and "joyful" appear in the English Standard Version of the Bible 430 times, while "happy" and "happiness" appear only ten times. As Christians, we've been given something that cannot be taken away—joy, which comes when we have the grace of Jesus Christ within us. We can rejoice no matter how many grumpy people or troubles we face, because God is *always* with us, as Nehemiah 8:10 (NIV) tells us: "This day is holy to our Lord. Do not grieve, for the joy of the Lord is your strength."

Isaiah 55:12 (NIV) promises, "You will go out in joy and be led forth in peace; the mountains and hills will burst into song before you, and all the trees of the field will clap their hands." Even when our circumstances appear dire, Isaiah reminds us in verse 61:10 (NIV) to rejoice in the Lord, "for he has clothed me with garments of salvation and arrayed me in a robe of his righteousness."

A stanza in **I'm Feeling Fine** refers to praying on our knees in the night so we can wake in the morning feeling fine. Problems will always face us, but when our joy is in the Lord, we can persevere and prevail. We just need to lay our worries and anxieties at the feet of Jesus—and leave them there.

My mornings start best with the Word of God and a cup of coffee. What about you?

> Heavenly Father, when we feel helpless and blue, remind us You are here with us, that You have planned a joy-filled life for us. We want to start and end our days with You. Amen.

Message..._____

_____

_____

Memory..._____

_____

_____

Music..._____

_____

_____

*Movement*_____

_____

_____

Day 15

I Know A Man Who Can

Words and Music by Jack Campbell
and Jimmie Davis

"You're so gullible, so naïve."
"Why would you do that?"
"I give you a year, maybe two, and you'll be back!"

So-called friends and family members wagered on how long we would stay once we moved from our city life to the country. Looking back now over forty-plus years, I admit I wondered the same myself. I must have been a little naïve or madly in love to follow my husband to sixty acres of hills, knowing he had never driven a tractor before. *What* were we thinking?

Do you ever have those same thoughts, wondering, "What am I *doing*?" Nowadays, we hear a constant cacophony of opinions. Strangers and people we barely know bombard us with their causes and their views on social media, trying to be the loudest and flashiest to get our attention and, often, our money. Don't you want to yell, "Stop! Leave me alone!"

More than enough opinions, including my own, fly through the airwaves. I'm reminded of Job and his three friends, Eliphaz, Bildad, and Zophar, who were full of opinions and advice for him while Job was in the midst of serious misery. Responding to their attempts to rationalize his trials and troubles, this man of God reminded them, "To God belong wisdom and power; counsel and understanding are his" (Job 12:13, NIV).

I'm discovering that only one voice, only one opinion, really matters: God's. When Momma introduced this song to me, she was clear about its potent message: we should *always* turn to this friend of hers, Jesus, for wisdom, consolation, and direction. No one else.

Next time you feel overwhelmed and scratch your head with a "Huh?" and wonder, "What am I *doing*?" remember, **I Know a Man Who Can** take your heartaches and anxieties and lead you to His rest. This friend of ours, Jesus, will help when no one else can.

God listens. God cares. God's followers trust in His wisdom and counsel. We need to stay in God's Word as we walk in this world. So, the next time a friend asks our opinion, let's respond with God's Word, not ours. We have no better place to be than in the center of God's will.

> Heavenly Father, guide me to seek Your wisdom rather than others'. Let me live in a way that others will want to come to know You. Make my life a testimony to Your goodness and faithfulness. Amen.

Message..._____

_____

_____

Memory..._____

_____

Music..._____

_____

*Movement*_____

_____

_____

Day 16

I'm Building A Bridge

Words and Music by Lee Roy Abernathy

One thing I know for sure: drywall dust, stacks of lumber, and wallpaper hanging from the ceiling are not ideal conditions for the homecoming of your precious newborn baby. We excitedly planned for our first child, who would also be the first grandchild and the first great-grandchild. My husband and I attended all the Lamaze sessions and practiced the techniques. The baby shower was checked off our "to-do" list. We chose a neutral paint color, yellow, for the nursery. (This was back in the old-fashioned days before new parents knew the sex of their baby before the birth.) But then our carefully laid plans were blown off course. Our baby was born before his due date.

Shocked that things didn't go precisely as we planned, we rushed to the hospital. All the grandparents huddled around the waiting room for more than fourteen hours, eager for this bundle of joy to arrive. When he finally entered the world, our relief was short-lived. Complications required us to stay hospitalized longer than we expected. Once that shock wore off, I concerned myself with worries about what that nursery would look like when we brought our baby home.

Not missing a beat, my Uncle Ray stepped up and took charge. He was a man of few words, but mighty in his work. He was more than a skilled wood artisan; he was a skilled craftsman of the heart. He worked tirelessly until that nursery was perfect, ready for the newest member of our family to come home.

After our hospital discharge, he and his young son, Tom, greeted us with a huge, *Welcome Home, Jason! (And Mommy, too)* banner. That topped any billboard sign I've ever seen. Uncle Ray was a builder extraordinaire, and **I'm Building a Bridge** was one of his favorite songs. He always requested I sing it just for him, and of course, I always obliged.

I recently read a quote attributed to Saint Francis of Assisi that describes my Uncle Ray completely: "Preach the gospel at all times. Use words if necessary." God was Uncle Ray's Master Builder, and he, like the Apostle Matthew, believed Jesus, when He said, "Anyone who listens to my teaching and follows it is wise, like a person who builds a house on solid rock" (Matt. 7:24, NLT). I can hear Uncle Ray asking us the same question at the end of this chorus: "I'll make it somehow, but how about you?"

> Heavenly Father, thank You for people like Uncle Ray, who show us how to build bridges to You. Please give us the skills and tools to follow his example, establishing a firm foundation with Your help. Amen.

Message..._____

_____

_____

Memory..._____

_____

Music..._____

_____

*Movement*_____

_____

_____

Day 17

I Wouldn't Take Nothing
For My Journey Now

*Words and Music by Charles
Goodman & Jimmie Davis*

B ack in the 1980s, our three sons spent many happy hours
reading the *Choose Your Own Adventure* series. Each book
offers a variety of outcomes, and readers determine the ending
they like best. The boys loved making their own choices,
controlling the story's outcome. The characters' fate depended
on them.

Seems to me this is an analogy for our walk with the Lord.

We make countless choices in our own adventures, some of
which lead us to dead ends. Amazingly, some people choose to
stay stuck there. But God gives us countless opportunities for
do-overs if we turn to Him for wisdom and guidance.

God's Holy insight, woven throughout the Bible, helps us
make optimum choices. The entire Book of Proverbs offers a
guide through every imaginable situation. *Laziness*: "Do not
love sleep or you will grow poor" (20:13, NIV). *Honesty*: "The
one who hates bribes will live" (15:27, NIV). *Child-raising*: "The
Lord disciplines those he loves" (3:12, NIV). *Morals*: "There
are six things the Lord hates, seven that are detestable to him:
haughty eyes, a lying tongue, hands that shed innocent blood,
a heart that devises wicked schemes, feet that are quick to rush
into evil, a false witness who pours out lies, and a person who

stirs up conflict" (6:16-19, NIV). Proverbs 31 even describes in great detail "The Wife of Noble Character."

Philippians 4:8 (CSB) sums up the collective wisdom of Proverbs and gives a road map to a happy ending for our own stories: "Brothers and sisters, whatever is true, whatever is honorable, whatever is just, whatever is pure, whatever is lovely, whatever is commendable—if there is any moral excellence and if there is anything praiseworthy—dwell on these things."

Despite God-given advice, I've stumbled, and I've been humbled. I've suffered heartache, grief, and woe. But, like the author of **I Wouldn't Take Nothing For My Journey Now**, with the Lord's help, I plan to stay on the path that will end in Heaven. What about you? In Psalm 34:4 (CSB), David reminds us that God is always ready to rescue and redirect wayward souls: "I sought the Lord, and he answered me and rescued me from all my fears."

> Heavenly Father, thank You for being the guiding light in our lives, offering us Your Word and counsel, providing us with a constant beacon in times of darkness. You have provided a straight path if we're willing to stay on it – and forgiveness when we stray. Keep us ever mindful of the happy ending You have planned for our lives: eternity with You and Your Son, Jesus Christ. Amen.

Message..._____

_____

Memory..._____

_____

Music..._____

_____

Movement_____

_____

Day 18

Until Then

Words and Music by Stuart Hamblen

Have you found yourself so frightened you feared your next exhale might be your last? Perhaps you've heard a grim diagnosis or lost your employment or been wounded by a family member who used you as a verbal punching bag.

I have experienced all these circumstances. The most devastating was my husband's diagnosis of Stage IV brain cancer in 2004. He was a healthy man! The week prior to his emergency brain surgery, he had baled hay in the fields and stacked it in the barn. Suddenly stripped of his strength and stamina, he was hospitalized, operated upon, and forced to relearn simple tasks.

In the days after his surgery, I felt as if I had to breathe for us both. Each breath held the weight not only of his future, but also our family's future. The decisions and adjustments I faced overwhelmed me, and I cried out to God, "How long, Lord? I can't do this anymore!"

Initially, I feared that the questions and anger I directed at God were signs of my faltering faith and weakening trust. But the more I reached out to God and dug deep into His Word, the more I understood I was in good company.

The prophet Habakkuk also demanded to know "How long, O Lord, must I call for help? But You do not listen!" (Hab. 1:2, NLT). I felt his pain and echoed his questions. Habakkuk knew the power of a faith renewal and how easy it is for anyone to fall away from faith when times are difficult.

Instead of asking "Why?" we need to ask "How?" King David told his son, Solomon, "Be strong and courageous and do the work. Do not be afraid or discouraged, for the Lord God, my God, is with you. He will not fail you or forsake you" (I Chron. 28:20, NIV). When we feel terrified and alone, we must trust the truth that God is with us always, everywhere, and He will never fail us. In our weakness, God's strength is revealed.

The Apostle James has an answer for us when we wonder how long we must endure our troubles: "Be patient, then, brothers and sisters, until the Lord's coming" (Jas. 5:7, NIV). **Until Then,** when worries and stress seem overwhelming, remember that God walks with us through all our trials and troubles—and He has a plan for us.

> Heavenly Father, help us cling to You as Habakkuk did in the midst of dark times. Remind us that nothing happens that You aren't aware of, and that everything happening in our lives is intended to draw us closer to You. Thank You for your constant presence and help. Amen.

*Message...*_____

_____

_____

*Memory...*_____

_____

*Music...*_____

_____

*Movement*_____

_____

_____

Day 19

Without Him

Words and Music by Mylon R. LeFevre

I couldn't breathe. I couldn't think or function. I never anticipated that my husband would die at an early age. I was astounded and distressed that my life wasn't going the way I had expected. What could I do? I felt lost, abandoned, hopeless.

Naively, I had believed that my husband would take care of me forever. Never did a thought of brain cancer, serious disabilities, and then premature death enter my mind. The cancer diagnosis struck us both with the realities of life and death. We had been living as if we would live forever. Until that moment, we were convinced that we had our lives well under control.

During the last years of my husband's life, we discovered new ways of living and caring for each other. After the stark realization that we were not in control, we learned to reduce our expectations and just do our best every day. And that was good enough. We grasped the hand of God and found genuine truth, love, and compassion. The **truth:** "Yet you do not know what tomorrow will bring. What is your life? For you are a mist that appears for a little time and then vanishes" (Jas. 4:14, ESV). Christ enveloped us in His **love:** "For God so loved the world, that he gave his only begotten Son, that whosoever believeth in him should not perish, but have everlasting life" (John 3:16, KJV). And His **compassion** never failed us: "The steadfast love of the Lord never ceases, his mercies never come to an end; they are new every morning" (Lam. 3:22-23, ESV).

Without Him, without Jesus, we truly would have been lost. Jesus walked with us through our Valley of the Shadow. But I admit worries and concerns flooded my mind after my husband's passing—and they probably echoed the feelings of betrayal and loss Christ's followers experienced after His death. They believed Jesus would save them from the Roman tyranny and create a utopia for them on earth. Similarly, I had believed my life on earth would follow *our* plan. In the months and years that followed my husband's death, I learned otherwise. We are part of *God's* plan.

How about you? Are you holding onto things and people of this world instead of clinging to the hand of God? This world and all that is in it are temporary, while God and His promises are eternal. "Choose for yourselves this day whom you will serve," Joshua advised the Israelites (24:15, NIV). We need to do the same.

> Heavenly Father, may we always be living testimonies to Your truth, love, and compassion. Teach us to live each day joyfully, without worldly expectations, with our eyes focused on You and Your promises. Amen.

Message..._____

_____

Memory..._____

_____

Music..._____

_____

*Movement*_____

_____

Day 20

Precious Memories

*Words and Music by J.B.F. Wright
and Lonnie B. Combs*

I'm addicted to HGTV. I especially enjoy the series *Home Town*, with Ben and Erin Napier. Their commitment to architectural preservation and interior design inspires me. In each episode, they share precious memories of the families who once called those houses home. They have made a firm commitment to improving the lives of their community and its people.

The show makes me wonder about my farmhouse. In years to come, what will people say about those city people who bought the farm in the mid-1970s? Will they guess how excited we were when the plat map finally recorded "Freeman" as the landowner? Will they chuckle when they hear about the city girl marching up to the local feed store and asking, "What do chickens eat?" Will they raise an eyebrow when they learn that the new landowner of these sixty acres had never driven a tractor before the purchase?

Paging through old photo albums with my granddaughters one day, I described our wall phone with the rotary dial and the party line we shared with our neighbors. "Didn't people listen to everyone's conversations?" they asked. I said we were respectful of each other's privacy—unlike these days, when people are unhappy if they aren't "liked" or "followed" by masses on social media. It seems everyone wants everyone to know everyone else's business.

Times do change, and moments turn into memories.

God gives us **Precious Memories** He wants us to cherish: the moments we spend with Him. Time spent in His Word and in prayer feeds our souls, as King David noted in his old age with a grateful heart. Psalm 71:5-8 (NLT) affirms his lifelong confidence in God's protection and provision: "O Lord, you alone are my hope. I've trusted you O Lord, from childhood. Yes, you have been with me from birth; from my mother's womb, you have cared for me. No wonder I am always praising you! My life is an example to many because you have been my strength and protection. That is why I can never stop praising you; I declare your glory all day long." David's life and his psalms are a litany of his most **Precious Memories**.

In verse 15 of the same chapter, David models what we should do with our own **Precious Memories**: "I will tell everyone about your righteousness. All day long, I will proclaim your saving power, though I am not skilled with words."

> Heavenly Father, with grateful hearts we thank You for our own **Precious Memories**. We pray that we will continue to develop a deep, loving relationship with You. We rejoice knowing that You offer us the same trust, hope, strength, and joy You offered mighty King David. Amen.

Message..._____

_____

Memory..._____

_____

Music..._____

_____

*Movement*_____

_____

Day 21

Just Any Day Now

*Words and Music by Eddie Crook
and Aaron Wilburn*

"Don't let me miss her," my husband always said as I carefully positioned him in front of the stage where our granddaughters would perform. Brain surgery had cost him the left peripheral vision of both eyes. When he walked, I walked beside him, protecting him, so he didn't bump into anyone or anything. He knew I not only had his back, but his left side as well.

Since his passing, I realized the greater meaning of his words. Yes, I don't want to miss anything my grandchildren do, either—I am a proud Mimi! But I am also a child of God who sees the signs of Christ's reappearing "each time I stop and take the time to look around me," as **Just Any Day Now** notes. What is in your field of vision?

In I Corinthians 13:12 (MSG), Paul acknowledges, "We don't yet see things clearly. We're squinting in a fog, peering through a mist. But it won't be long before the weather clears and the sun shines bright! We'll see it all then, see it all as clearly as God sees us, knowing him directly just as he knows us!"

How can we bring clarity to our vision? "Seek ye first the kingdom of God, and His righteousness; and all these things shall be added unto you," Matthew 6:33 (KJV) tells us.

After Jesus reveals His approaching death, He comforts His disciples. "Don't let your hearts be troubled. Trust in God,

41

and trust also in me." He promises, "When everything is ready, I will come and get you so that you will always be with me where I am" (John 14:1,3, NLT).

When will that day come? Will everyone I love be ready? Jesus reassures us just as He did His disciples: "Do not worry about tomorrow, for tomorrow will worry about itself. Each day has enough trouble of its own" (Matt 6:34, NIV).

My husband trusted me to position him for clearer vision. We need to do the same for others, reminding them of Christ's promise: "I am the Way, the Truth and the Life. No one can come to the Father except through me" (John 14:6, NLT). We don't want to stand in someone's way, so they can't see Him. We want to show them the way.

> Heavenly Father, touch our eyes and help us see clearly. Touch our hands, so we may point others to You. Remind us as we watch and wait, that we need to tell others about Your love and grace along our journey. In Jesus's name, we pray. Amen.

*Message...*_____

_____

_____

*Memory...*_____

_____

_____

*Music...*_____

_____

_____

*Movement*_____

_____

_____

Day 22

Where No One Stands Alone

Words and Music by Mosie Lister

I sail out of a peaceful slumber, listening for the birds' reveille outside my window and the rustle of covers from the other side of the bed. The clock announces the time is 5:33 a.m. But I don't hear any sound. Is this a dream?

No. I have a new reality now, waking alone. No nudge. No whisper. An empty pillow beside mine. The silence of mornings is deafening. The loneliness is consuming. It leaves me depleted and unmoored.

For years, my husband struggled with the repercussions of exposure to Agent Orange from his days as a soldier during the Vietnam era. He died following years of chemotherapy and radiation. During my season of caregiving, I appreciated all the support I had from family, friends, health care providers, and hospice. I certainly wasn't alone on this journey. Yet it was immensely difficult to witness him slipping away. We both knew our adventure together was ending too soon.

The cliché "Where God guides, He provides" certainly described our journey. In the moments I felt alone, even when surrounded by medical experts, I could envision the Great Physician guiding them and me along the next steps. As my husband took his last breath while I cradled him in my arms, I knew we weren't alone. God was with us, **Where No One Stands Alone.**

But then I faced the great void. I was living by myself for

the first time in my life, lost and without direction. I turned to Deuteronomy 31:8, (NIV): "The Lord himself goes before you and will be with you; he will never leave you nor forsake you. Do not be afraid; do not be discouraged." Even now, I can slip into the fear of abandonment, but I turn to the Word for solace.

I know many of you have suffered a significant loss: a spouse, close friend, family member. You, like me, might need a daily—or hourly—reminder that "Where God guides, He provides." Memories can serve us in two ways: they provide a reflection of what was and a reminder of who we are in Christ. If we trust in the God who knows and loves us, He will anchor us in His loving care, especially when our seas are rough.

So, when our feathered friends sound reveille, let's start every day rejoicing in God's love. We are not alone. In this season of our lives, perhaps God is calling us to be the reveille for someone else who feels alone.

> Heavenly Father, You know the agony of watching Your precious Son die on the cross, so You understand our deepest despair, desperation, and loneliness. We bring them to You, asking You to fill the void with Your love. In Jesus's name, Amen.

*Message...*_____

_____

*Memory...*_____

_____

*Music...*_____

_____

*Movement*_____

_____

Day 23

Tears Are A Language God Understands

Words and Music by Gordon Jensen

"Don't cry, Mimi!" my granddaughters said. As they ran from the stage and into my arms, they knew they would be showered with hugs, smiles, and tears. Can't help myself. When they questioned my tears, I quickly reassured them, "These are happy tears. My heart is smiling so much I can't keep it inside."

In this season of life, my tears run the gamut from happy to sad. Grandchildren bring so much happiness. A sudden memory brings sadness—a small plane flying overhead reminds me of my husband's love for flying. Then more tears fall as I think about our sons taking over the farming business without him. I am sad at what I've lost, but so grateful for those I love and have loved.

God doesn't discount or forget any of our tears. In Psalm 56:8 (ESV), King David tells God, "You have kept count of my tossings; put my tears in your bottle. Are they not in your book?" Not a restless night or cry for help goes unnoticed by our God, *El Roi* (The God Who Sees). The chorus of **Tears Are a Language God Understands** echoes David's thoughts: "He sees your tears and hears them when they fall." I can't hear the sound a tear makes when it falls, but God can. He is that close, holding our hands and promising always to be with us.

Repeatedly, God acknowledges our sorrows. In Isaiah 25:8 (NIV): "He will swallow up death forever. The Sovereign Lord will wipe away the tears." In Jeremiah 31:16 (NIV): "'Restrain your voice from weeping and your eyes from tears, for your work will be rewarded,' declares the Lord." Yet even "Jesus wept" (John 11:35). Remember? The shortest verse in the Bible is perhaps the most powerful and personal to me. Jesus knows and acknowledges our heartaches. He comforts us, He even cries with us because of His indescribable love for us.

Revelation 7:17 (NIV) promises, "God will wipe away every tear from their eyes." Can you picture God Himself gently brushing the tears from your eyes? One day, the Lord will call His faithful followers home, to a place where no tear will ever fall, a place where we will be covered with smiles as we are reunited with our loved ones.

> Heavenly Father, thank You for understanding the language of our tears, and for loving us so deeply that You record our tears while we are here on earth. We are so grateful for the promise of a blessed, tear-free eternity with You. You know our heartaches and feel our anguish and pain. May we show the same compassion to the people we see every day. Amen.

Message..._____

_____

_____

Memory..._____

_____

Music..._____

_____

Movement_____

_____

_____

Day 24

The Love Of God

Words and Music by Frederick M. Lehman

"He said he loved me. Why did he do this?" Have you heard a friend say these words? Or perhaps you have uttered them yourself. Love, defined by this world, is fickle. We hear love is blind; love is tender; love is true; love is adulation. Yes, love is all those things and much more, but those words don't begin to define **The Love of God.**

My parents introduced me to a deep and abiding love. I was the center of their universe, enveloped in a cocoon safe and joyful—but even their love can't compare to **The Love of God.** Hundreds of Scripture references describe God's love. The words of the chorus remind us that God's love is rich, pure, measureless, powerful, strong, and eternal. Nothing can remove us from His love.

Psalm 103 in *The Message* reads, "God is sheer mercy and grace not easily angered; he's rich in love. He doesn't endlessly nag and scold, nor hold grudges forever. He doesn't treat us as our sins deserve, nor pay us back in full for our wrongs. As high as heaven is over the earth, so strong is his love to those who fear him. God's love, though, is ever and always eternally present to all who fear him" (vs. 8-11,17).

My love for my family and friends is deep and powerful, but I can't possibly imagine giving one of my sons' lives for someone who hates and reviles him. Yet God offered His Son to save a world full of sinners, and Christ willingly sacrificed

His life for us. "God demonstrates his own love for us in this: While we were still sinners, Christ died for us" (Rom. 5:8, NIV). Only God can offer such complete sacrificial love. Not even my parents could rival His love for all of us.

"HE said HE loved me. Why did HE do this?" We cannot begin to measure the depth and breadth and height of God's love for us—a love so great that His sacrifice redeems us. I can only be awed and immensely grateful. His love is not fickle, it is forever. His love is not blind, it is revealing. His love is not exclusive, it is available to all who believe.

> Heavenly Father, we are so very grateful for the love You showered on us. We stand on Your promises to love us fully, unconditionally, and eternally. We know that nothing can ever separate us from Christ's love. "No... overwhelming victory is ours through Christ, who loves us" (Rom. 8:37, NLT). May we always sing praises to Your name. Amen.

Message..._____

_____

_____

Memory..._____

_____

_____

Music..._____

_____

_____

Movement_____

_____

_____

Day 25

When He Was On The Cross,
I Was On His Mind

Words and Music by Mike Payne & Ronny Hinson

Emails. Facebook. Computers. Televisions. iPads. Cellphones. Instagram. Google. Round-the-clock newscasts. In today's intrusive world, I struggle to concentrate and find time to think without distractions. Do you? Social media especially seems to interfere with any original thoughts of my own. When that happens, I know it's time to take a complete break.

Deep breathing exercises and stretches help me silence my world's cacophony. Even better is spending time digging into God's Word instead of other people's lives. As a child, I memorized Psalm 46:10 (NIV), "Be still, and know that I am God." It often becomes my mantra, as it soothes my soul. Eugene Peterson's paraphrase in *The Message* offers a 21st-century version of this verse: "Step out of the traffic! Take a long, loving look at me, your High God, above politics, above everything."

God instructs us to fill our minds and thoughts with *Him*, not personalities, politics, or pleasures.

The message in **When He Was on The Cross, I Was on His Mind** amazes me. Our God, who reminds us to "take a long, loving look at Him" today, was thinking of you and me even in His darkest hour when His Son was dying on that cross.

We can't hide from God. The Creator of the universe knows all our thoughts, feelings, and needs. Psalm 139:4-5 (NLT) reminds us, "You know what I am going to say even before I say it, Lord. You go before me and follow me." God hears our worries, our concerns, our darkest thoughts, and secrets—so why not discuss them with Him directly? He loves us! We can trust His advice, counsel, and direction.

When He is on our minds and in our prayers, we grow to understand His plans for us. When we "take five" from the noise of the world, we can find time and energy to use the unique gifts and talents He gave us to bring glory to His Kingdom and peace to our souls.

Which of your unique talents are silenced by the constant din around you? How can you use them for Him today?

> Heavenly Father, help us to stop, look, and listen. Help us think about You in all we do, knowing that You were thinking of us even when Your Son was dying on the cross. Help us make quiet time for quiet talks with You. Only then can we hear Your thoughts, plans, and intentions for us in this noisy, chaotic world. Amen.

Message..._____

_____

_____

Memory..._____

_____

Music..._____

_____

Movement_____

_____

_____

Day 26

What A Day That Will Be

Words and Music by Jim Hill

Have you ever had a day when you wanted to throw the alarm clock against the wall and crawl back into bed? I have! And I've also wished or worried entire days away, with nothing to show for them except crumpled tissues and chocolate wrappers.

Sometimes a good cry helps the situation. But some days I wrestle with anxiety and exhaustion instead of turning to God and His Word for peace and strength. I recently re-read the story of the Old Testament prophet Daniel and his friends. When they found themselves facing calamities, they relied upon the only one who could help—God. They bypassed their own wisdom and advice from others and went straight to the source of all answers. As a result, "Daniel handled the situation with wisdom and discretion" (Dan. 2:14, NLT).

How often do we wring our hands, wandering from friends to professed media experts for solutions, when we need to follow the example of Daniel and his friends, who fell on their knees in prayer whenever they faced crises— and there were many. When God provided solutions, Daniel immediately responded, "I thank and praise you, God of my ancestors, for you have given me wisdom and strength" (Dan. 2:23, NLT). Too often I try my way first, and only when that fails do I turn to the Almighty. Can you relate?

Seemingly endless days of questions and unease will

disappear when we see Jesus. **What A Day That Will Be**! Never again will we cry. Never again will we experience sickness or loss or pain. We will see His face, and we will *rejoice!*

Keeping that day in mind helps me face today. Less frequently do I ask, "Why did this happen?" More often, I feel assured God knows what is happening in my life and He has a plan for me. That's what matters. All my days belong to Him. I belong to Him. And He loves me.

When that day comes, and it will, God won't ask about the condition of our homes, our finances, our families, or our careers. He will ask us what we have done with our lives, if we have told others about Christ and if we have modeled Christian assurance and love.

Until then, God offers us His peace, strength, and wisdom.

> Heavenly Father, every day is a blessing from You. Every day is an opportunity to reflect Your love, Your caring, Your compassion, and Your message. Help our unbelief and give us the assurance of Your will in our lives. We look forward to the day we see You face to face. Amen.

Message..._____

_____

_____

Memory..._____

_____

Music..._____

_____

*Movement*_____

_____

_____

Day 27

I've Been Changed

Words and Music by Mosie Lister

I've Been Changed. This was Daddy's song and the story of his life. Every time Momma sat at the keyboard and began playing the prelude, Daddy would stand up, tap his thigh to the rhythm, and belt out the words.

My father was born in the backwoods of the Great Smoky Mountains. He grew up in a log house filled with lots of children requiring lots of chores. Whenever I heard stories about hauling moonshine and drag racing around curves on those treacherous mountain roads, I wondered how he ever survived his adolescence.

My father often said he always knew he wanted more out of life. He thought heading north to Michigan would be the answer. But that wasn't the solution to what he really needed. Daddy needed Jesus. And when Daddy met his Jesus, he went to the river to be baptized, knowing his sins would be washed white as snow. As the song lyrics say, he wandered for years, lost. And then he was found.

In the parable of the Prodigal Son, a wayward son returns home repentant, and his father rejoices the way God rejoices whenever one of us turns—or returns—to Him. "'For this my son was dead, and is alive again; he was lost, and is found.' And they began to celebrate" (Luke 15:24, ESV).

Towards the end of his life, Daddy struggled to stand and speak, but whenever he heard my mother tickle those ivories on her piano keyboard, playing **I've Been Changed**, Daddy could stand a little taller and pat his hand on his thigh, smiling as I belted out the words for him. The devastating effects of Alzheimer's disease did not rob him of the healing and encouraging power of music—nor did it rob him of his God.

This song will forever bring tears to my eyes and a smile to my face. I know my Daddy is standing in the presence of God, giving thanks to the Lord for all that He has done. I know that the heavenly host celebrated my father's baptism—and ours—with overflowing joy. How about you? Do you need to turn to God with a deep and abiding need? Is there a song that brings back the memory of the moment you realized that you, like my father, needed more in life?

> Heavenly Father, I am grateful for Your grace. Thank You for finding us. May we ever be aware that You sought us, and when You found us, You rejoiced. May we all feel Your love in a special way today, the way my father did whenever he heard **I've Been Changed**. Amen.

*Message...*_____

_____

_____

*Memory...*_____

_____

*Music...*_____

_____

*Movement*_____

_____

_____

Day 28

One Day At A Time

*Words and Music by Marijohn
Wilkin & Kris Kristofferson*

During my father's memorial service, our pastor read *The Dash Poem*, written by Linda Ellis. Its message is brilliant in its entirety; it echoes the sentiment in 1 Peter 1:6-7 (NIV): "You may have had to suffer grief in all kinds of trials. These have come so that the proven genuineness of your faith—of greater worth than gold, which perishes...—may result in praise, glory and honor when Jesus Christ is revealed." The poem, like the Apostle Peter, reminds us not to cling to earthly treasures in our short years—our dash—on earth.

My father was a wonderful man whose life wasn't always easy. But he always tried to make everyone else's life a little easier and brighter. His smile was infectious, his love for my mother and me indisputable. I adored him.

His eighty-plus years, the stretch referred to in *The Dash Poem*, defined who he was. Daddy lived his "dash" well. He loved his Savior, his family, and southern gospel music, particularly when performed with Momma on the keyboard and me singing one of his favorite songs. His dash was filled with stress and joy, fun and failures. Unfortunately, his later years were marred by the dreaded disease of dementia.

During those last months of his life, Daddy helped me understand the essence of embracing the moment. When

Momma played the piano, his smile glowed. And my Daddy laughed a lot. As we walked and I talked, he stopped frequently and smiled kindly at a cat drinking water from a birdbath, at a passing stranger, or at one of nature's beauties. He reached for the flowering blooms on the low branches of nearby trees, smelled them, and smiled. I often wondered if they reminded him of his days growing up in the Great Smoky Mountains.

I think perhaps his last gift to me was the gift of time, the realization that every single day is infinitely precious. The words of the song **One Day at a Time** remind us, *"Pushin' and shovin', crowding my mind; so for my sake, Lord, teach me to take one day at a time."* I must stay in the moment. Worries about the future or regrets about the past do nothing but rob us of the present.

What about you? Do you cling too much to the past or worry about the future and forget to live for today? Psalm 118:24 (NLT) reminds us, "This is the day the Lord has made. We will rejoice and be glad in it."

> Heavenly Father, help me appreciate every single day. Help me to stop and smell the spring blossoms, watch Your sunrise, listen to a bird sing, and appreciate the hint of snow in the air on a frosty winter day. Show me Your way, **One Day At A Time.** Amen.

Message..._____

_____

Memory..._____

_____

Music..._____

_____

*Movement*_____

_____

Day 29

Whatever It Takes

By Lanny Wolfe

Is there a prayer you are afraid to pray? Are you frightened God might just answer that one? I know God answers our prayers in His own inimitable yes-no-maybe fashion, but something in the words of the song **Whatever It Takes** terrified me.

My spiritual résumé was decent. I could pull it out anytime I needed it. I came to know Christ at an early age. I went to church, memorized Scripture, taught Sunday School, led Bible studies, sang in the choir, et cetera, et cetera. I had a lot to show for my faith in God—but the invitation to "draw closer to me" haunted me.

I'm afraid I was one of those Christ-followers who stood at a distance. I was doing good things, after all, but for whose glory? His? Or mine? After all, I didn't have time to draw closer. I had a family to raise, a career to pursue. I had already met Christ at the foot of the cross. I knew the Lord's Prayer. Isn't that all I needed? So, those words *must* be for someone else. Right?

I worried if I prayed the prayer "Whatever it takes, Lord," it might just come true. Yet look more closely at the lyrics. The message is for *believers*. Those of us who know Christ as our Savior are the ones who should desire a daily closeness to God. I had allowed my family, my career, my possessions, my calendar, and my will to interrupt my fellowship with Him.

I came to understand that my prayers are not just wishes, like blowing the candles out on your birthday cake. The most important prayer I can utter, following that of salvation, is seeking to be in the center of His will moment by moment.

I Peter 4:11 (NIV) instructs us, "If anyone speaks, they should do so as one who speaks the very words of God. If anyone serves, they should do so with the strength God provides, so that in all things God may be praised through Jesus Christ. To him be the glory and the power forever and ever." To *Him*—not me—be the glory!

Author Lanny Wolfe had us in mind when he composed this song. God uses ordinary men and women—you and me—to do His extraordinary will in this world. God asks for a willing heart to follow Him.

> Heavenly Father, thank You for never giving up on me. You know what I need before I ask, and now I know You want me to draw even closer to You. I thank You for Your grace and constant presence in my life. Amen.

Message..._____

_____

_____

Memory..._____

_____

Music..._____

_____

*Movement*_____

_____

_____

Day 30

Look For Me At Jesus' Feet

Words and Music by Squire Parsons, Jr.

W hat does the future hold? Where will you be when you draw your last breath?

No one knows the answers to those questions. Like some of you, I've heard devastating diagnoses and prognoses. I've sat in an ambulance racing to the hospital. I've paced a hospital floor believing my mother's heart was so generous and full of love it couldn't possibly give out. But it did. As humans, we face countless challenges, from health concerns to financial woes, job losses, and troubled relationships.

Prepared? Never.

Not even the apostles were exempt from hardships. We all journey along paths riddled with obstacles. As Ecclesiastes 9:11-12 (NIV) warns, "The race is not to the swift or the battle to the strong, nor does food come to the wise or wealth to the brilliant or favor to the learned; but time and chance happen to them [us] all. Moreover, no one knows when their hour will come."

However, our lives are filled with a cloud of witnesses. We have "heroes of the faith," as the Book of Hebrews reminds us. Special people guide us and help us on our journey: Sunday School teachers, family members, ministers, Bible study leaders, and friends. The Apostle Paul wrote, "Therefore, since we are surrounded by such a huge crowd of witnesses to the life of faith, let us strip off every weight that slows us down, especially the sin that so easily trips us up. And let us run with endurance the race God has set before us. We do this by keeping our eyes on Jesus" (Heb. 12:1-2, NLT).

My mother kept her eyes on Jesus, witnessing through her life and her music. At a revival meeting years ago, a quartet sang **Look for Me at Jesus' Feet**. Mom whispered to a friend, "June, that's where I'll be. Look for me there!" My mother made it crystal clear where she would spend eternity. I'll know where to find her.

God wants us to *run* the race He has set before us, not sit on the sidelines. When we cross our finish line, we want to hear God say, "Thou good and faithful servant, welcome home."

> Heavenly Father, one day may we declare what my mother and the Apostle Paul could affirm: "I have fought the good fight, I have finished the race, I have kept the faith" (II Tim. 4:7, NIV). We want to live as heroes of the faith, able to tell others about Your love and grace and willing to help them on their paths. Let us proclaim, "Look for me at Jesus' feet." Amen.

Message..._____

_____

_____

Memory..._____

_____

Music..._____

_____

Movement_____

_____

_____

Day 31

How Great Thou Art

Swedish folk melody written by Carl Gustav
Boberg, translated by Stuart K. Hine

My family's most treasured hymn is **How Great Thou Art**. Any rendition—instrumental, soloist, choir, or *a cappella*—leaves us inspired, even spellbound. I saw George Beverly Shea mesmerize his audience when he performed this song during a televised Billy Graham crusade. The music and lyrics are stand-alone masterpieces.

Today, as I close my eyes, still my heart, and think of my mother playing **How Great Thou Art,** tears well up and a smile brightens my face. Momma made the rafters ring when she played during our church services, and the choir rose to meet her there.

I wonder if Mr. Boberg referenced Psalm 145 when he penned the words. Dozens of verses in the Bible tell of God's greatness, but Psalm 145:3 (NIV) tops them all: "Great is the Lord and most worthy of praise; his greatness no one can fathom."

Singing is what I love to do most, and some of the greatest hymns are based on verses in the Book of Psalms. Many psalms list authors' names and the occasions for writing; some offer liturgical notes and musical notations, even recommending appropriate instruments. The Book of Psalms originated with King David and was completed by the fourth century before Christ, yet the words speak to us as if the ink is still drying on the page.

Scholars believe that Psalm 145 is King David's last "song of praise." He urges us to praise God "for ever and ever" in recognition of His majesty, mighty acts, compassion, righteousness, faithfulness, and abundant goodness. When I remember that the Creator of the universe sent His own Son to save us, words fail me—but they never failed King David.

The fourth verse of **How Great Thou Art** offers me the peace and reassurance and a glimpse of the way my mother met Jesus, face to face: "Take me home, what joy shall fill my heart! Then I shall bow in humble adoration and there proclaim, my God, how great Thou art!" I am confident God took my mother's hand and led her home.

How about you? Is there a hymn that you treasure, one that expresses your hope in God? The final psalm, 150, begins and ends with a constant reminder to us all: "Praise the Lord!" Music is a marvelous way to do so.

> Heavenly Father, I pray that these devotions bring us the confidence and joy we can only find in You, as we journey through life. You have showered us with remarkable blessings. We come to You with open hearts and complete trust that one day, You will lead us home. Amen.

Message..._____

_____

Memory..._____

_____

Music..._____

_____

Movement_____

_____

Biblical Translations

All Scripture is given by inspiration of God, and is profitable for doctrine, for reproof, for correction, for instruction in righteousness…That the man of God may be perfect.
II Timothy 3:16-17 (KJV)

I've grown in my spiritual walk with the Lord since I began reading a variety of translations. My first Bible was the King James Version, which I love. But each translation gives me a fresh perspective on God's meaning and purpose, and you'll see that I make use of many different translations when I seek God's wisdom.

Revised Geneva Translation (RGT)
The Geneva Bible was the very first widely distributed version of the Holy Bible in English, and it was Shakespeare's favorite translation; it preceded the KJV by fifty-one years. The RGT is a 21st-century update of the Geneva Bible, specifically designed to be spoken and heard. This translation is based on the belief that a crucial key to revival occurs when we *speak* God's Word eloquently. The RGT preserves the textual cadence and poetry that is typical of Elizabethan literature, while eliminating archaic and potentially distracting 16th-century words, phrases, and punctuation.

King James Version (KJV)
The King James Version is the world's most widely known Bible translation. Authorized by King James I of England, it was published in 1611. Its powerful, majestic, musical style reflects God's glory. A literary classic, many of its phrases and expressions long ago became embedded in our everyday speech.

New King James Version (NKJV)
Published in 1982, this is a modernization of the King James Version of 1611, using the same underlying Greek text for the New Testament. It preserves the KJV's dignified style and the musicality of its word and phrase order but replaces some words and expressions that are no longer easily understood.

Revised Version (RV)
Working together, British and American scholars produced the Revised Version in the 19th century after the discovery of ancient manuscripts that clarified aspects of biblical scholarship. The New Testament was published in 1881, the Old Testament in 1885. The first substantive revision of the King James Version, the RV served as the basis for the American Standard Version of 1901.

English Standard Version (ESV)
A team of more than 100 leading evangelical scholars and pastors worked together to produce the ESV, which was released in 2001. They based this translation on William Tyndale's 16th-century New Testament, the KJV (1611), English Revised Version (1885), American Standard Version (1901), and the Revised Standard Version (1952 and 1971).

New American Standard Bible (NAS)
The New American Standard Bible is a literal translation from the original texts. It follows the style of the King James

Version, but uses modern English for words that are no longer commonly used or whose meanings have changed. It uses capital letters for pronouns relating to divinity, as I have done throughout this devotional. ("There He sat down with His disciples.")

New English Bible and Revised English Bible (REB)

Working together, the major Protestant churches of the British Isles initiated a new translation of the Bible in the mid-20th century, relying on the best Hebrew and Greek texts to present the writers' full meaning in clear modern English. The New Testament was published in 1961, the Old Testament in 1970, and a significant revision was published jointly by the University Presses of Cambridge and Oxford in 1989.

New International Version (NIV)

The most widely used of any modern Bible version, the New International Version focuses on meaning-for-meaning principles with word-for-word translations in straightforward, contemporary language. First published in 1978 by Biblica, it includes in-depth footnotes and commentaries.

New Revised Standard Version (NRSV)

An ecumenical team sponsored by the National Council of Churches thoroughly revised the original RSV and published the NRSV in 1989. The translators used contemporary biblical manuscripts to clarify obscure passages. It uses gender-inclusive language, identifying where the original texts include both males and females.

New Living Translation (NLT)

Ninety leading Bible scholars translated the New Living Translation in clear contemporary English, relying upon the ancient texts with a goal of "the Truth made clear." Published in 1996, this version often clarifies meanings (for example, "disreputable sinners and corrupt tax collectors").

The Message (MSG)

Eugene H. Peterson published *The Message: The Bible in Contemporary Language* in segments between 1993 and 2001, as a personal paraphrase of the Bible using contemporary American slang.

Christian Standard Bible (CSB)

The Christian Standard Bible (CSB) is a major revision of the 2009 edition of the Holman Christian Standard Bible (HCSB), which was released ten years earlier. The CSB incorporates advances in biblical scholarship to improve translation decisions, word choice, and style. It also removes some of the innovations of the HCSB; it consistently translates the Greek as "Lord" rather than "Yahweh" and uses "brothers and sisters" for the plural term "brothers."

Biography: Jackie Freeman

Jackie Freeman loves words. Words that inform. Words that inspire. Speaking, singing, reading, and writing words. And she loves to make a joyful noise to her beloved Lord and Savior.

Her love of reading and writing blossomed as a child when her grandmother, Nettie Thomas, introduced her to literature. Her home had a marvelous collection of books, from stories by Louisa Mae Alcott to Margaret Mitchell, Zane Grey, and Mary Jane Holmes. Jackie's passion for words started at her grandmother's bookcase. Years later, she joined writers' groups to hone her skills.

A Siena Heights University graduate, Jackie specialized in early childhood education. While serving as an adjunct at her alma mater, she also became an assistant principal of a Montessori school, and later served as the Early On Coordinator for Saline Area (MI) Schools. She left that position to become a full-time caregiver, first for her husband and then for her parents.

Jackie and her husband raised their three sons on a sixty-acre farm in southeast Michigan. She is a doting grandmother who loves pickleball and co-authored *BEND YOUR KNEES, LOUISE!* a children's pickleball primer. She is a gifted vocalist and loves singing, whether in a church, an auditorium, beside the sickbed of loved ones, or outdoors in nature. She frequently speaks and sings at women's retreats and church events.

To learn more about Jackie Freeman, go to:
www.jackiefreemanauthor.com

|||||||||||||||||||||||||

9 781664 247796

CPSIA information can be obtained
at www.ICGtesting.com
Printed in the USA
LVHW021520090222
710691LV00025B/375

9 781664 247796